The Asian Elephant

Written by Guo Xianming, Jiang Zhicheng, and Chen Jinsou   Illustrated by Xia Tian and Sun Heyu

SEE Noah's Ark Biodiversity Conservation Book Series

Preface

The Southwest Project Center of the Alashan Society of Entrepreneurs & Ecology (SEE) initiated a program in 2013 for biodiversity conservation of the alpine forests in China's mountainous Southwest. Named SEE Noah's Ark, it is financed by the SEE Foundation in Beijing. Multiple conservation projects have been implemented by working with various stakeholders to protect endangered and rare species of flora and fauna, especially those with extremely small populations. It adopts solutions inspired by nature and advocates participation by the community, encouraging protection and the sustainable use of local biological resources.

The stories in the SEE book series: *The Asian Elephant*, *The Yunnan Snub-Nosed Monkey*, *The Green Peafowl*, *The Fish of the Jinsha River*, and *The Himalayan Honeybee*, all come from true experiences of front-line rangers and locals in conservation action. They are incredible. For both nature's characters and the people in the story, their connection to the native land and affection towards each other is rarely heard and miraculous in their own way. We then came up with a proposal to compile these lovely stories in a picture book to all our friends who have supported SEE conservation projects. They can be linked to real characters from dense woods and remote mountains, where heart touching stories occurred due to their generous support.

This picture book series is a group of works by conservation workers, scientists, sociologists, writers, and artists. The characters, environment, and neighboring creatures have all been carefully selected from real situations in our projects. In addition, explanatory notes of conservation are made to enrich the reading experience. We hope you enjoy it!

We extend our respects to those who have worked so hard to conserve their natural homeland, as well as to the SEE members and public who give donations to support these projects. These volumes are our gifts for the United Nations Biodiversity Conference COP15 held in Kunming.

XIAO JIN
Secretary of the SEE's Southwest Project Center
Chairperson of the SEE Noah's Ark Committee
June 2021

Data File: Asian Elephant

Name in Chinese	亚洲象 (YAZHOUXIANG)	Order	Proboscidea
Name in English	Asian elephant	Family	Elephantidae
Alternate Names	Indian Elephant, Great Elephant, Wild Elephant	Genus	*Elephas*
Latin Name	*Elephas maximus Linnaeus*	Species	*Elephas maximus*
Kingdom	Animalia	Subspecies	7 Seven
Phylum	Chordata	Distribution	China, Southeast Asia, South Asian Tropics
Subphylum	Vertebrata	Authorship	Linnaeus, 1758
Class	Mammalia	Conservation Status	(EN) IUCN Endangered
Subclass	Eutheria		

Distribution and Conservation Areas in China

Autonomous Prefecture/City	County/District	Conservation Areas and National Parks Constructed
Pu'er	Simao	Yunnan Pu'er Sun-River National Park
	Jiangcheng	—
	Jingdong	Ailao Mountains National Nature Reserve
	Jinggu	—
	Ning'er	—
	Lancang	Nuozhadu Provincial Nature Reserve
Xishuangbanna Dai Autonomous Prefecture	Menghai	—
	Jinghong	Xishuangbanna National Nature Reserve
	Mengla	Xishuangbanna National Nature Reserve
Lincang	Cangyuan	Yunnan Nangun River National Nature Reserve

The Xishuangbanna National Nature Reserve spreads out over the entirety of Xishuangbanna. It includes the Mengyang Sub-Reserve, Menglun Sub-Reserve, Shangyong Sub-Reserve, Mangla Sub-Reserve and Mangao Sub-Reserve. Xishuangbanna Dai Autonomous Prefecture contains the Naban River Watershed National Nature Reserve and Yiwu Prefectural Nature Reserve.

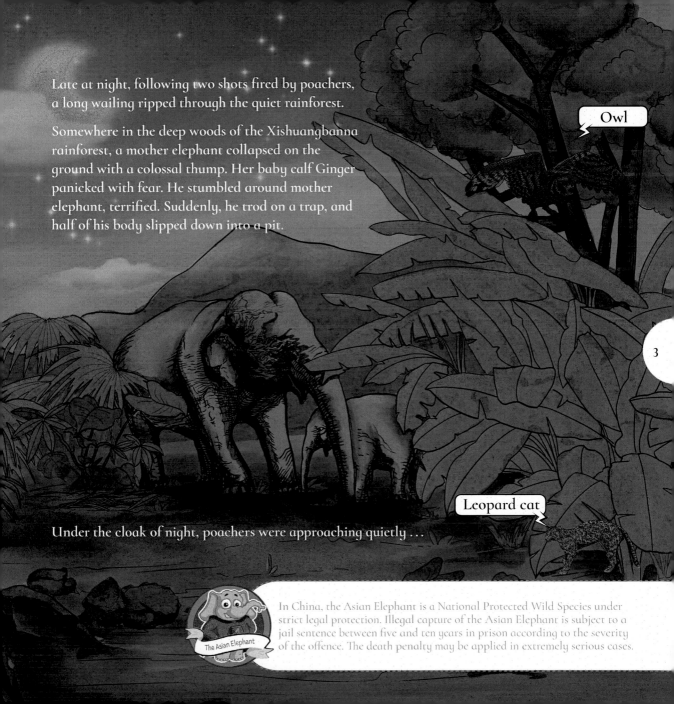

Late at night, following two shots fired by poachers, a long wailing ripped through the quiet rainforest.

Somewhere in the deep woods of the Xishuangbanna rainforest, a mother elephant collapsed on the ground with a colossal thump. Her baby calf Ginger panicked with fear. He stumbled around mother elephant, terrified. Suddenly, he trod on a trap, and half of his body slipped down into a pit.

Owl

3

Under the cloak of night, poachers were approaching quietly ...

Leopard cat

The Asian Elephant

In China, the Asian Elephant is a National Protected Wild Species under strict legal protection. Illegal capture of the Asian Elephant is subject to a jail sentence between five and ten years in prison according to the severity of the offence. The death penalty may be applied in extremely serious cases.

Seeing her calf in the trap, frightened and struggling, mummy elephant, with her last strength, slid into the pit and pushed Ginger out of the trap with her long trunk. The calf took the chance to use his strength to break free.

Ginger turned his head and looked back. His mom collapsed on the ground. The whiff of rifle gunpowder and the sounds of the hunters' footsteps were approaching. With mom's trunk pointing the direction and pushing, Ginger moved into the dense forest nearby in a panic.

Giant lizard

The Asian Elephant

Asian Elephants are entirely grey or grey combined with a brownish red. Their thick skin with many folds and sparse body hair provide them protection in the dense rainforest. Male adults have lengthy tusks, a weapon for self-defense and mating fights, and a good tool for scraping away tree bark. Their trunk is the longest of all living animals and is an extension of the nose connected with the upper lip, made up of over 4,000 muscle fibers with a rich nervous system. It is not only highly sensitive to smell, but also operates as a tool for collecting food, drawing water, and a powerful weapon for self-defense.

Little Ginger lost his mother. He drifted around the rainforest alone. Not a single herd was willing to take him in. Ginger became an elephant wanderer – all on his own.

He remembered how his mom held up grass with her trunk, to drive the mosquitoes away from him. He remembered midday naps, sprawling his body over her trunk. But the memory of that dreadful evening frequently haunted him, the appearance and smell of the poachers, and how they shot his mommy.

He wanted to grow up quickly, and take revenge for his mom!

6

White heron

Crested serpent eagle

The Asian Elephant

Asian Elephants generally live in herds. Each herd contains from a few to a dozen elephants. Each community is made up of mothers and their young children. The females are leaders. When the male elephants reach around 14–20 years old – sexual maturity – they leave the herd and live alone or with other males.

Ginger strayed around, living a lonely wanderer's life, wary of any tiny movement around him and weighing every step. Ginger was frightened of falling into another trap.

8

With his memory, Ginger went to places where his mom used to take him to look for food. But all had changed. Dense groves of rubber trees had taken the place of those gentle slopes. Others were now terraced tea plantations and the wild bananas were gone. All Ginger could smell was the pungent whiff of fertilizer over the farmed banana plantation.

As years passed, Ginger found food in fewer places. He went hungry for more and more days.

Sooty-headed bulbul

The herbivorous Asian Elephant consumes more than 300 types of plants in their habitat in China. An adult male consumes between 150–250 kilograms of food a day. So elephants stroll between 18–20 hours every day in food searching, only sleeping for 2–4 hours. Threats to the elephant's survival come from extensive human land exploitation for plantation, destroying their habitat. In addition, much of their food supply has been reduced because the natural succession of rainforest vegetation in the rescues becomes too dense for herb plants to grow.

The Asian Elephant

9

One day, while out scouting for food, Ginger wandered out of the forest and found himself in a thick cornfield. The crispy and juicy corn was simply delicious! He ate as much as he could, to his content. He hadn't been full in a long, long while.

As his belly was full, Ginger rolled on the ground in the cornfield. He lay down and had a lovely midday nap.

But a sudden rumbling and thundering startled him awake.

The Asian Elephant

Given its huge body, the Asian Elephant must eat continuously to keep itself warm. But foods in the wild are widely dispersed and ripe in different seasons. Elephants also consume a lot of energy while gathering food. Sugarcane plantations and farm crops provide them with high calories to readily meet their daily needs. That is why elephants come to graze the fields frequently during the harvest season, which is when elephant-human confrontation peaks.

There in the distance, Ginger saw someone lighting firecrackers, and someone else beating the gong. The enormous bangs and loud noise of the firecrackers agitated Ginger and he felt angry. It reminded him of the gunshots that night . . .

Revenge!

12

Pi-pa!
Pi-pa!

Ginger, grown up and massive,
rushed madly towards the people.
They scattered, terrified.

13

Asian Elephants are strongly territorial and keep alert to the surrounding environment when foraging. Intruders will be driven away by the herd together. When human beings try to drive them away from their fields and villages through fire, beating drums and gongs, and firecrackers, the Asian Elephants, frightened into self-defence, would attack in groups. Elephants, having been previously injured or having seen a human bring harm to one of their family members, may keep the memory. They will most likely take revenge if the chance comes.

The Asian Elephant

Furious with rage, Ginger pushed over a wooden hut, and smashed the side of a tractor.

14

15

Wild Asian Elephants are large-sized mammals that can be ferocious and highly aggressive. They are unlike domesticated elephants. Despite their size, they can run at speeds of up to 36 kilometers per hour over short distances, which is far quicker than most human beings. People are unlikely to escape in a short-range attack. Taking precautions to avoid such an encounter is the best way. Or keeping a safe distance. According to long-term observations and research conducted by front-line staff, that distance should be at least 200 meters.

Having indulged himself down in the cornfield, Ginger didn't ever want to go back to those sporadic foods in the forest.

Ginger made his day wandering around villages in the sugarcane plantations and cornfields. He also stomped straight into the cottages and kitchens. He turned over sacks of corn and salt, enjoying some ready-made treats.

Ginger's biggest worry now was the steel wire wrapped around his hind leg. It was swollen, and the wire was sinking into the muscle. The pain was almost unbearable.

The Asian Elephant

Most animals need salt to supplement their diet to balance internal circulation. Plants have a very low salt content and elephants occasionally take rocks or mud containing minerals to meet their needs. Asian Elephants are highly sensitive to the smell of salt. One whiff is enough to attract them, and they will put their trunks in and gorge on all the lovely flavors.

Burmese python

Until one day, the swelling finally made it impossible for Ginger to stand up.

Feeling pain and despair, Ginger spotted a human figure approaching. That terrifying memory of his mother's agony came pouring back. Ginger roared with desperation.

Suddenly Ginger fainted. He lost all consciousness ...

19

Established in 2008, Yunnan Asian Elephant Breeding and Rescue Center is China's only research base for elephant rescue and breeding.

When he came to himself, Ginger saw that the wire on his leg had gone, and a thick salve had been applied to his swollen leg.

"That human? Could it be – that he saved me?"

Pretty soon, Ginger's right hind leg healed up.
He could take a longer journey foraging.

Vietnam mouse-deer

The Asian Elephant

Historically, Asian Elephants were distributed widely over China, with their footprints found across half the country's territory. Fossil evidence shows the elephant reaching as far north as Anyang in Henan. The animal went extinct in south Fujian around the 12th–13th century and disappeared from Lingnan and Guangxi around the 17th century. From then on, they could only be found in Yunnan, with a population of around 300 along the Southern Gun River in modern Xishuangbanna, Puer, and Lincang. This is a number smaller than the Giant Panda, making the Asian Elephant a Class I animal on the List of Endangered and Protected Species of China.

Ginger stumbled upon a place called Lotus Pond, inside the nature reserve's boundary. He looked over. Around was elephant grass (*Pennisetum purpureum*) spread all across the hills, and the tigergrass (*Thysanolaena maxima*) and wild bananas (*Musa acuminata*). It was just like being back where he and mom used to go scouting for food. Everywhere he smelt his favorite and familiar foods.

Ginger was happy to walk among this elephant food. He caught sight of many old friends from the forest. There was the Indian wild ox, the sambar, the red muntjacs, wild boars as well as jackals. It was like everybody found this paradise – and everybody loved being here with Ginger!

23

Long-tail shrike

The Asian Elephant

Yunnan has set up several nature reserves to ease conflicts between elephants and men. An entire area is reserved as a source of natural foods for the Asian Elephant, with thick patches of planted tigergrass, wild bananas, and bamboo that Asian Elephants love. Mineral licks are set up for the complementary diet. These areas are called "Elephant Canteens." This creates a livable habitat, to attract the Asian Elephants back to their natural environment, in order to keep them from intruding into human production and residential areas.

Ginger found that some people were moving in the area around the Elephant Canteen. He realized they were clearing the poachers' traps and dreadful wires.

Ginger was a little confused. So just what are human beings? – enemies or friends? Should I still take revenge?

Silver pheasant

One day, he caught a whiff of a young female elephant's scent. He heard her cry out.

Red muntjac

The Asian Elephant

The Asian Elephant is an iconic rainforest species. It is also seen as the "engineer" of the rainforest. Its enormous frame shuttles between the trees, clearing paths. Clumps of bamboo fall over as elephants harvest them. That creates a window so that the sunshine can get through tree crowns, into the thick shades of the dark forest. This allows the rainforest to sustain its health, and creates iterations for rainforest plant life, as well as for the activities of medium-sized and small animals. Elephant footprints form small puddles, which are habitats for rainforest amphibians and for hydrophilic plants to thrive. Elephant feces provides nutrition for seeds to sprout and for soil bacteria – even bacteria find a home there!

Ginger followed the scent all the way, until he caught sight of a young female elephant, who was trapped in a narrow water reservoir. She twisted and turned in anxiety.

26

The Asian Elephant, symbolically, is deeply rooted in the cultures of many of Yunnan's ethnic minorities. The Mekong River, the only Asian river to flow through six Southeast Asian countries, known as the Lancang River in Chinese, is known as "The River of a Million Elephants" in the Dai ethnic language. In Dai mythology, legends, toponyms, poems, language, dance, paintings and sculptures, all featuring elements connected to elephants, have become an important symbol of its tradition. Elephant worship reaches a peak in Wa ethnic culture, with its reference to elephants as "Da" or "Dading," meaning elder or ancestor.

The Asian Elephant

Keeping at a distance, Ginger watched the people use a bulldozer to help the girl out. Finally, a gap opened up! The young lady elephant climbed out of the reservoir.

Great hornbill

Ginger hurried up to greet the young flustered, female elephant and led the way towards the Elephant Canteen. When the young female had examined Ginger – big and tall, handsome, nice white tusks – she felt secure. She ran behind Ginger, feeling at ease, and off into the forest.

28

About the Authors

Guo Xianming, senior engineer. He graduated from Yunnan Forestry University in 1989 and joined the Xishuangbanna National Nature Reserve the same year. He has been working in biodiversity investigation and monitoring in the Reserve for a long time and has held and participated in the construction of a biodiversity monitoring system and comprehensive scientific investigation of the Reserve. His current work focuses on Asian elephant protection and research, and he has presided over many projects, including the Asian elephant protection project, the Asian elephant monitoring system construction project, the Asian elephant habitat restoration, and food source construction project, etc. He has published and participated in more than sixty papers and six monographs.

Jiang Zhicheng received his bachelor's degree in Ecology and his master's degree in Zoology from Yunnan University between 2012 and 2019. The Cornell University Environment Education Outcome also authenticated him to complete the third wildlife diversity infrared camera technology training and the China Biosphere Reserve Network member training under the Chinese National Committee for Man and Biosphere Programme, UNESCO. He has published five papers (one in Chinese Core Journals and one in SCI) and participated in one monograph.

Chen Jinsou graduated from the tailing's engineering and management department at Kunming Metallurgy College in 2013. He joined the SEE Project Center in 2018 and engaged in green peafowl and Asian elephant protection works.

About the Illustrators

Xia Tian received his bachelor's degree in costume design from Yunnan Arts University and his master's degree in information technology engineering from Wuhan University. In addition, he has studied visual communication at Tongji University. He is the founder and general manager of Kunming Benpu Culture Communication Co., Ltd. and an external tutor at Yunnan University of Finance and Economics.

Sun Heyu received her master's degree in the art of design from Yunnan Arts University. She is now an assistant professor in the department and vice president and professional leader at the Yunnan Vocational College of Culture and Arts. She has held and participated in multiple research projects and published many papers in authoritative journals.

SEE Noah's Ark Biodiversity Conservation Book Series

SEE: The Asian Elephant

Written by Guo Xianming, Jiang Zhicheng, and Chen Jinsou
Illustrated by Xia Tian and Sun Heyu

First published in 2023 by Royal Collins Publishing Group Inc.
Groupe Publication Royal Collins Inc.
BKM Royalcollins Publishers Private Limited

Headquarters: 550-555 boul. René-Lévesque O Montréal (Québec) H2Z1B1 Canada
India office: 805 Hemkunt House, 8th Floor, Rajendra Place, New Delhi 110 008

Original Edition @ Yunnan Science & Technology Press Co., Ltd.

ISBN: 978-1-4878-1084-9

To find out more about our publications, please visit www.royalcollins.com.